I0021769

Samsung Galaxy
Note 10 &
Note 10 Plus
User Guide

Simplified Manual for Unlocking the
Samsung Galaxy Note 10 & Note Plus
in 30 Minutes

Benjamin F. Trigger

Copyright© 2019

This book is dedicated to all Samsung Galaxy Note 10 users/owners

Contents

INTRODUCTION

Did you just buy a Samsun note 10 or Note 10 Plus? Big congratulations! After unboxing your brand new Samsung Galaxy Note 10, and Note 10 Plus, there's a whole lot to learn about the device. This book will help you get the maximum bang for your Galaxy NOTE 10 device.

You'll learn how to set up your device easily, navigate the touch-screen and customize your home screen, customize the notification Panel, customize your camera settings, and browse with the world's first phone with an ultrasonic fingerprint sensor built.

These tips and tricks will help you optimize the ownership of your smartphone.

You will learn about the best settings you need to change on your brand new Samsung galaxy Note 10 and Note 10+ to make it better.

You'll also be getting tips for troubleshooting the Galaxy Note 10.

PART 1

SETTING UP THE GALAXY NOTE 10 PLUS

The all-new Galaxy Note 10 Plus and Galaxy Note 10 Plus are the newest and fanciest of Samsung smartphones released. But to be fair, there are a lot of fantastic smartphones Samsung released to us this year. But with a big battery of 4,300 mAh. the Note 10 Plus is now the talk of Samsung's town.

The Note 10 Plus is a lot different from the Note 9. And of course, you get a whole new color. You have the Aura glow, Aura black and the Aura white. The Galaxy Note 10 Plus is fitted with a 6.3 inch FHD+ screen. This is a tad smaller than the one you find in Note 9.

But the Note 10 Plus breaks the bank being 6.8 inch Quad HD+. The edges of the device are slightly more rounded and you also have the fingerprint sensor giving the device more functionality and a seamless feel and look.

The Note 10 Plus and the S10 Plus are the greatest phones Samsung released this year. But you don't want to get them confused. Not only do they look different, but their abilities also differs

The Galaxy S10 Plus has a 41,000 mAh battery while the Galaxy Note 10 Plus is armed with a 4,300 mAh. But on a recent test, the battery for the S10 Plus actually outlasted the Note 10 Plus.

It's crazy because we all though a higher mAh means longer battery life. But the thing is that the Note 10 Plus has a bigger OLED screen and a lot of features for the S-Pen. These are all big things for the battery to power. As a result, even though it's got higher mAh, it powers a lot of things so it's bound not to last as long as the S10

Another difference is that the Galaxy Note 10 Plus has a storage of 256 GB. It's an incredible amount of storage and only if you don't take videos every day, it's going to take years to fill it up. But the S10 Plus only comes with 128 GB. To be honest, however, 128 is already more than enough.

Then when you talk of size and weight. The Galaxy Note 10 Plus has a length of 6.4 inches while the S10 Plus is just about 6.2. Weight for the Note 10 Plus is 196 grams while S10 Plus is left with 175 grams. While both phones look beautiful, the fact that the Galaxy S10 Plus is lighter than the Note 10 Plus makes it a bit more recognizable when you hold it.

The Samsung Galaxy S10 is a great phone, it's very big and it's got the latest upgrade for a

Galaxy. Plus it's even got the S-Pen. But there's more to the devices than its size and beauty. In the following sections, we'll be talking about how you can fully maximize the use of your Note 10 Plus.

PART 2

TIPS, TRICKS &
TROUBLESHOOTING

How to customize Bixby routines in Samsung Galaxy 10 Plus

A new feature that's available to new Samsung phones is the Bixby routines. This is just like IFTTT which means If This then That. If all this sounds new to you, Routines allow you to set different actions that will be triggered by just one action.

1. Enter the **Setting**
2. Choose **Advanced Features**
3. Select **Bixby Routines** to set up a routine
4. You should see set routines available but if you want to set up your own, use the + icon at the corner
5. Set a name for the routine
6. From the list shown, select a trigger
7. Choose your car's Bluetooth device
8. To choose an action, select **Next**

9. Hit the **+** button to select actions again.

Force close apps on the Samsung Galaxy Note 10 Plus

The process of force closing an app on your Galaxy Note 10 Plus is pretty straight forward. But there are 2 ways to go about it. The easiest and quickest way is to go through the Recent Apps sections. To do this,

1. Press the Recent Apps soft key when you are on any screen (this is the button just next to the home key by the left.)
2. The recent apps should show up now, you can close specific apps. Or if you want to free your phone entirely, you can just close all apps at once.

This should close all apps in the background. But it doesn't do a deep force closing. If this process doesn't get you what you want, here's the second method

1. Enter the **Settings**

2. Choose **Apps**

3. Select **More Settings** (this is the 3-dot icon at the upper right section)

4. Choose the option for **Show System Apps** Find that app that you want to close and select it

   Choose the **Force Close** button

While this method is not as straightforward and quick as the first one, it's is likely to stop any issue and problem that is caused by an app.

Digital Wellbeing on the Samsung Galaxy Note 10 Plus

With the new Android release, there came a ton of new features. These features give way to whole new possibilities we never thought of. One of these features is the Digital Wellbeing tool by Google. This tool was created to help users of the Android understand how they usually interact with their devices.

The main goal of this feature is to help people get a balance between the real world and the digital one. It's a pretty brilliant innovation because when you take a look at the street, bus park, coffee shop, everyone is burying their heads in their phones. You narrate an hour-long experience to a friend and when you're done he looks up and all he asks is 'what were you saying?'

With all the commotion, the digital wellbeing can allow users to get an overview of how they use their device, they can see how much they use some apps and how frequently they check their phone.

To see the breakdown of how you use apps

1. Enter the **Settings**
2. Touch **Digital Wellbeing**
3. Select **Dashboard**
4. Tap so that you can see the Times Opened, Screen Time and Notification Received
5. You can also check Apps Overview

Using secure folder on the Samsung Galaxy Note 10 Plus

The secure folder feature was released to Galaxy Note devices a while ago. Now the Galaxy Note 10 Plus enables you to use its feature. To those who have no idea what the secure folder is, it functions just as the name implies; it's a folder that keeps your things secured.

This feature uses the Samsung Knox technology to store apps, data, and other information you would rather keep private.

You can also move data from native apps to the secure folder. The data and apps kept in the secure folder are individually sandboxed. This is done so that they are isolated completely from the rest of the data or apps stored on the device.

And of course, with all the technology, not just anyone can access this folder. For others aside from you to gain access to this area, they will need the personalized lock type you set. If you would like to set this up, here's how

1. Fire up the app drawer and enter the **Secure Folder** app. You will then get information about the perks of this feature

2. You have to sign in to your account and also configure lock type options. This lock type will be used to unlock this folder

3. When you create it, the secure folder will be presented to you. With the option to **Add App**, you can store an app separately from the normal one used already.

Split screen apps on the Samsung Galaxy Note 10 Plus

You can use Multiwindow if your Note 10 Plus makes use of stock Android. You just have to swipe up from the lower part of the display. You can also tap the upward arrow at the bottom taskbar. The screen should split into two hence the name Split Screen. You just need to add an app to both sides and you're well on your way

1. Move to the home screen of your Samsung device
2. From the bottom of the screen, swipe up. Or touch the arrow at the middle of the taskbar
3. Open an app you'll like to use slide it to the left area
4. Open up another app you'll like to use and slide to the opposite area.

The screen will be divided into equal 50 / 50 parts. But you're not restricted to this, if you want to get one part bigger than the other, you can just use the vertical divider to expand. So when you expand the right screen, the left will of course, get smaller.

Take Ultra Wide photos on the Samsung Galaxy Note 10 Plus

If a phone doesn't have a good camera, it's not going to sell much. One of the biggest selling points from companies is cameras. But Samsung doesn't need to shout about how sharp and awesome their cameras are, we all know it is quality.

But what there we are jonesing for is the new feature for their devices to take Ultra-Wide photos. Not many phones give you this feature. In fact it's possible to count these phones in a few minutes. The feature does just what the name says. (Is it just me or is Samsung really good at naming things.)

This feature makes your shots, not just wide, but really Ultra Wide. You just have to shoot with your camera. It's only when you see it that you'll understand how wide things can get. And the thing is that you can do just fine with the normal camera setting. But when you arm yourself with the Ultra Wide camera, you get the fish eye effect to your photos. Though some are not big fans of this, you can easily fix it in the Settings

To use the Ultra Wide camera, fire up the camera app. You'll find three icons beside the bottom of the view finder. Use this to switch to Ultra Wide

How to use AR Emoji on the Samsung Galaxy Note 10 Plus

This is a good one for those who really love to take selfies. Your Samsung Galaxy Note 10 Plus is able to take AR Emojis. What this does is that it turns your face into an emoji. Though the image will be in cartoon form, it will definitely have a semblance to you.

When you take an AR Emoji, you can then share it with friends through Messages

If you would like to take an AR Emoji of yourself, here's how you do it.

1. Fire up the **Camera** app
2. Choose **AR Emoji**
3. Select the option for **Create My Emoji** and you may need to select **Allow**

4. Instructions will be pasted on the screen to help you capture the emoji, when it's done and set, hit **Capture**.

5. Choose a body type you love and select **Next**

6. Now you may notice that things don't seem quite right with the emoji. You have the option to edit the emoji before you save it and it goes live. Hit the **Edit** button at the top right corner

7. Make your changes and when you're done, save your emoji with the **check mark**

Scene optimizer on the Samsung Galaxy Note 10 Plus

Scene optimizer is also another new feature. It's one of the recent additions Samsung made to their Galaxy Note line. The name doesn't give much away about its abilities. But what it really does is that it increases your photo quality.

It is an AI feature that studies the object you're trying to capture and does all the needed changes to boost the quality of the photo and give you that sweet image.

If you would like to enable this option, you just have to
1. Fire up the **Camera** app
2. At the top left area of the screen, tap the **Setting**
3. You'll see the first option for **Scene Optimizer**, toggle this on.

4. Now when you point your camera at an object, you will see a blue icon. Very quickly, the object will be recognized and changes will be made accordingly.

How to customize home screen

The lock screen and the home screen of your galaxy device are like the most important area for almost everyone. And the fact that you can customize it to suit your taste is all the more thrilling. If you would like to change the setting for your Note 10 Plus device,

1. Swipe upward when you are in the home screen. This action will open up the app drawer
2. Select **Settings**
3. Select **Display**
4. Hit **Home Screen**
5. These are the settings you can change in your home screen
   - Home screen grid size
   - Home screen layout
   - App screen grid size
   - App icon badge

- Apps button lock home screen layout
- Swipe down for notification panel
- Add apps to home screen

How to transfer data from old device

There's a solution that Samsung has provided to assist their users to change from their previous note device and still get their data. This is the Samsung Smart Switch. You can use this to switch phones without delay.

1. Install the **Smart Switch** app on your Samsung devices. You can easily find this on the Play Store.
2. Put your 2 Galaxy Note device side by side and open up the app on both phones.
3. On the old Note device
   - Select **Wireless**
   - Choose **Send**
   - Then **Connect**
4. On the new Note 10 Plus,
   - Select **Wireless**
   - Choose **Receive**

5. Your old note device will use its technology to look for the Note 10 Plus.

6. When devices are connected, you will then need to choose the content you would like to send to the new Note 10 Plus device. Choose the items and hit **Send**.

How to efficiently use the navigation settings

Of course, you get the normal button navigation settings on your Note 10 Plus but you are still granted to make some changes. If you'd like to change the navigation bar,

1. Enter the **Settings**
2. Choose **Display**
3. Select **Navigation Bar**
4. When you are in the menu, you can choose the order for your buttons. You may even wish to switch to the order that other devices use.

How to use Dual Messenger

1. Fire up the **Settings** app

2. Choose **Advanced Features**

3. Scroll down and select the **Dual Messenger** option

4. You will be presented with social media apps. You can just toggle the one you'd like to use Dual Messenger for.

5. If you would like to use the same contacts list across your accounts, leave the **Use Separate Contact List** option disabled. If you want separate contact list, enable it

6. When you enable Dual Messenger, the app's twin will show in the apps drawer. And don't worry, you will be able to tell them apart.

How to customize the email notification Settings

If you would like to customize the notifications and alerts for emails on your Note 10,

1. Select **Application**
2. Choose **Email**. You want to make sure that the email account shown in the inbox is one you're looking to edit. If it's not, select your account name at the upper left area and choose desired account
3. Hit the **Menu**
4. Select **Settings**
5. Press **your email address**
6. Tap or clear the Email Notification check box under **Notification Settings**
7. Choose **Select Ringtone**
8. Pick the ringtone you'd like to use
9. Select **Vibrate** and tap the check box to enable

Setting up fingerprint scanner for security

The fingerprint scanner for the Note 10 is unlike the ones you find in other galaxy phones. This one is powered by working with sound waves and this is reflected on the skin. With this, the device can detect your finger even when it's packed with grease, dust, water, lotion or even when there's just too much light available.

With the high tech sensor embedded, a 3D image of the finger will be taken and all the ridges, slops and wrinkles of your skin will be detected so that it can be identified when you try to unlock with it. If you are thinking of setting the sensor up, you are making a great move in guaranteeing your security. Here's how you set it up

1. When you are in the home screen, swipe and reveal the apps screen
2. Enter the **Settings**
3. Go to **Biometrics and Security**, then **Fingerprints**
4. When you are in **Fingerprints**, enter in your password, PIN or pattern. It just depends on the one you currently use.
5. If needed, select **Continue**. Choose a lock screen option. This can be a password, PIN or pattern. Go through with the steps to finish up the process.
6. If needed, select **Continue** and register your fingerprint. You do this when you swipe your finger on the sensor. You may need to repeat this step till you've completed the process.
7. At the bottom right area, select **Done**
8. It's now time to turn on the **Fingerprint** switch. Use the toggle
9. With that, you just set up your fingerprint scanner.

Set up night mode

Just like the rest of the smartphones available today, you have the night mode feature on your Note 10 plus. It's great that phones are gearing toward this move because using your mode in normal mode at night can put quite a strain on the eyes. It is why you find it hard to sleep immediately you use your phone.

The Note 10 Plus has a dark mode feature that turns the interface into AMOLED black. Pretty sure you're not one who likes seeing a shiny white background light from your phone at night. You can turn the night mode on when you

1. Go to **Settings**
2. Chose **Display**
3. Select **Night Mode** and turn it on. It's also a good idea to set a schedule

Set up Edge Lighting

Again with the ability to name things, Samsung's Edge Lighting feature is a favorite of many. With the Edge screen on the Note 10, you get a ton of glows for your notifications. The default and normal lighting is the Basic and it's quite good.

To be sure, it does the job quite well and you can live just fine with it. But still, why settle for less when you can have everything. You can get a lot of effects and animations from the Edge Lighting styles and they just scream exquisite beauty.

1. Select the **Edge Screen**
2. Choose **Edge Lighting**
3. Hit **Edge Lighting Style**
4. You should also edit the kind of apps that can trigger Edge Lighting. Do this easily with the **Manage Notifications** option

Taking advantage of video & sound enhancer

When you have **Dolby Atmos** enabled on your device, you will notice that is sound will be louder. You start to think that the audio is coming from every spot in the entire room. To turn it on,

1. Fire up the **Settings**
2. Choose **Sounds And Vibrations**
3. Select **Advanced Sound Settings**
4. Tap **Sound Quality And Effects**
5. Choose the **Dolby Atmos** option to turn on the toggle.

If you would like to get the most out of your music, you can just select the text that reads **Dolby Atmos**. You are selecting the text not the toggle. You will be shown a page. This is where you can make your enhancement for Dolby atmos. You can just select Music to get the best of audio.

One-Handed mode

If you would like to use the One-Handed mode on the Note 10 device, here's how you enable it

1. Enter the **Settings**

2. Choose **Advanced Features**

3. Select **Motions And Gestures**

4. Select **One-Handed Mode**

5. From the options that shows up, choose your favorite and you're well on your way to using the One-Handed mode.

PART 3

TROUBLESHOOTING COMMON PROBLEMS

Fingerprint scanner issues

1. If you are using another protector apart from the built-in version, it's best you take it off now as that can be why you experience issues.

2. In fact, you can take it a step further and remove the built-in protector and check if there's improvement.

3. You can also move your finger around several locations on the fingerprint scanner screen. Don't hold the phone in one hand and use another hand to unlock the phone. Hold the phone in one hand and unlock with that same hand. It's only normal that way.

Accidental touch problems with the Note 10

We all know how massive the Note 10 Plus is. People would normally exclaim when they see the Note 10 but when they are presented with the 10 Plus, it's a different story. Not only is the device big, it's also got some extra slim bezels.

There's like nowhere to place your hand as you use the device as it would be like you're holding the screen itself. This is why some experience accidental touch issues.

You can disable this with the settings

1. Enter the **Settings**
2. Choose **Display**
3. Move down and tap **Accidental Touch Protection**
4. Turn on the switch

Fix the no app drawer button

This one is not a direct issue but some really need the real app drawer button. Those coming from older generation phones will be shocked when they see no app tray icon, physical button or home key button.

The apps button you can definitely get back

1. Hold down any empty area of the home screen. You will find the display zooming out and bring you a set of options to edit.
2. Select the **Settings** icon. This is the just like your normal gear settings shaped icon.
3. Choose the **Apps Button** option
4. Choose **Show Apps Button**.

This device freezes

If you notice that some apps or the galaxy Note 10 itselft freezes all of a sudden or gets unresponsive, this is not the first time such is happening on a galaxy phone. It's common to experience this in the contacts apps you try to make a call

If you notice this, hold down the volume down and power buttons simultaneously for about 9 seconds. This will get the phone to turn off and begin afresh. Even if you find the phone frozen with a black screen, try this option

Wi-Fi GPS issues

It's common for new phones to have some kind of issues with Wi-Fi. A lot of things can cause this, but here are helpful solutions,

1. Forget the Wi-Fi network. As you know, this doesn't mean that you cannot connect to the network ever again.
   - Enter the **Settings**
   - Go to **Connections**
   - Choose **Wi-Fi**
   - Press and hold that Wi-Fi connection and select **Forget Network**

   You just have to find that connections again and connect to it.

2. Another good option is turn off the router then after, say, 10 seconds, turn it back on.

3. Don't let your Wi-Fi sleep
   - Enter **Settings** then choose **Connections**
   - Select **Wi-Fi**

48

- Tap **Advanced Settings**
- Turn off **Wi-Fi Sleep** option.

But if you use this option, you should know that apps can continue to use Wi-Fi.

Camera issues

The camera for the Note 10 is excellent and the only thing that can be considered as a problem is the fact the rear cameras don't switch to a specific lens. Not everyone will experience this but for those who do, it's a great option to reboot the phone.

Other minor thing that has been reported is very dark slow motion videos. But first of all, for the slow-mo feature to treat you well on the Note 10, you need to be in a place with a lot of light. If you do this inside the house, you won't be very pleased with what you get. So when you look at it, it really isn't a problem.

S-Pen issues

If your S-Pen is not obeying your orders, you can try to place it back in the phone. In minutes, it should be recharged and you can try using it.

Most of the problems you experience with your device can be easily fixed by restarting. Even the most experienced technician will recommend turn off and turning on. That's always been the go-to solution and it always will. We're in the 20 century but we still need some good old techniques to solve the problems of even the latest phones. Funny, right?

DISCLAIMER

This book is not an overall guide to all Note 10 Plus tricks and troubleshooting

ABOUT THE AUTHOR

Benjamin Trigger been writing tech related books for some 15 years now. Some of his research materials have appeared in international magazines and blogs.

www.ingramcontent.com/pod-product-compliance
Lightning Source LLC
Chambersburg PA
CBHW031248050326

40690CB00007B/1012